ANSWERING CHILDREN'S FAITH QUESTIONS:

Through Parable, Poetry, And Prayer

By Elaine M. Ward

DEDICATION:
    For Ann Beaty
        Who knows the power of parable, poetry, and prayer.

ANSWERING CHILDREN'S FAITH QUESTIONS:
Through Parable, Poetry And Prayer
By Elaine M. Ward
Copyright © 1999 Educational Ministries, Inc.
ISBN 1-57438-031-1

Educational Ministries, Inc.
165 Plaza Dr.
Prescott, AZ 86303
800-221-0910

Contents

Introduction   5

A. God

God is Creator   15
God is Parent   17
God is the Smile in Our Lives   19
God is Love   21
Where Is God?   23
Plans for Food, Flowers and Faith   25
God Is With Us   27
God Is the One Who Is With Us   29
Where Is God's Dwelling?   31
What is Heaven?   33
What Does God Require?   35
The Lord Is My Shepherd   38
The Still, Small Voice   40

B. Jesus

Jesus Loves and Welcomes Us   45
Jesus is Like a Good Shepherd   47
The Shared Christmas Gift   49

The Angels' Notes   51
After Advent: Jesus and the Rich Man   53

C. The Earth

Taking Care of the World   59
The World (and Well) Belong to God   61
The Earth is the Lord's   63
What I Can Do?   65

D. Other Faith Questions

What is Imagination?   69
The Answer Is In Your Hands   71
What is Baptism?   74
Bedtime   76
When I Am Afraid   79
Let Heaven and Earth Praise God   81
What is Pentecost?   83
What Happened on Good Friday?   85
Death   87
Why Do We Have to Die?   90
What is Easter?   92
What is Thanksgiving?   94
How Can I Help?   96
Why Do We Pray?   99

Introduction

"Finally, be strong in the Lord and in the strength of his power. Put on the whole armor of God, so that you may be able to stand against the wiles of the devil. For our struggle is not against enemies of blood and flesh, but against the rulers, against the authorities, against the cosmic powers of this present darkness, against the spiritual forces of evil in the heavenly places."   Eph. 6:10-20

uzanne's birthday is in November and when she turned six she took the train into the big city with her dad for a special birthday outing. She had a wonderful day. They went to the zoo, ate big chocolate sundaes, window shopped, and at the end of the day made the two-hour train trip home. It was dusk when they caught the bus from the train station to their street. It was quite dark and chilly when they started walking hand in hand the three blocks up Canner Street. There were no streetlights. Suzanne had been a big girl all day but now she felt small. "It's dark, isn't it, Dad." "It sure is." "But God will protect us, won't He, Dad?" "Sure..." "There isn't really a God, is there, Dad?" In that delicate moment, Dad's voice must have faltered. Suddenly the street seemed very dark indeed, and two small children continued hand in hand up Canner Street.

"In the dark" children, as Suzanne, ask the deep questions that cause us to falter. During the worship service, when the lights were dimmed and the church darkened, the five-year-old behind me asked his mother, "Why does it have to get dark?" Children have doubts in the dark. "Is there a God? Does God love me? Will God protect and care for me?" Prayer includes our doubts and fears, our confusions, complaints and questions. " How long, O Lord, how long?" questioned the psalmist. There are times the desert is so dry or the darkness devours us when we experience the silence of God. It is then we pray, "I do not know how to pray." The disciples did not say to Jesus, "Teach us how to pray," but "Teach us to pray."

Children ask questions all day long: "Where is God? Where is Grandma now that she is dead? Where did I come from? What is prayer? What's a Samaritan? Who is God? Why can't I see God now? Why did Jesus die? Why did Jesus have two fathers? Where is God? Why are some people poor and others not? Why are there wars, mosquitoes, and five toes rather than six?" At the bottom of all questions and answers about God, mystery, life, and death is the question "Is the universe friendly?"

All of us seek the meaning of existence and want answers and explanations. Who am I? Who are you? What is the Christian faith? What shall I do? I believe there are answers, but God's ways are not our ways. Being human we are not always able to understand, but God asks us to love rather than understand. Some things just are, whether we understand them or not. Therefore our "answers" become affirmations of love and trust in God who loves, rather than explanations. Sometimes our presence is the "answer," for Suzanne was less interested in a precise theological reply than one of assurance. "Am I safe in the dark? Can I trust this world?"

Helping children face disasters and the "dark" is a long-term process of "being there" to give responses, tell parables, participate in prayer, and even more, being there because our presence matters. Some children are blessed, as Suzanne, with a dad (or a substitute for dad) to hold their hand in the dark. God has given us the gift of imagination so that together with our faith we find "a hand" to hold. Asking and answering is a mutuality of relationship, a give and take of joint inquiry. Listening with love and respect means valuing the asker and appreciating the question and the child's search to know.

When we doubt, we raise questions. "There isn't really a God, is there, Dad?" Doubt keeps our dogmas and doctrines from decaying, from making an idol of our religion or our institutions. It celebrates freedom and responsibility, for where we have absolutes, we have no need of faith. Faith takes the place of knowledge.

Children who see and experience pain and suffering, loss and injustice, ask, "If God loves and cares, why doesn't God do something?" I remember a nurse asking that question by the bedside of a dying child and hearing the reply, "I did. I sent you."

A child asked her father, "What was God doing last night during the storm?" Then, answering her own question, she put God's love and care in perfect perspective. "I know. God was making the morning." In the midst of the crises of life, we can know that our loving Parent is not waiting to conduct the funeral of our hopes and dreams. God does not conduct funerals, God conducts resurrections, making all things new.

Some children do not believe in prayer. To them God may seem "dead" or abstract or too distant to hear, and for some God's "hands" are tied because of their own materialistic understanding of the world. Others, seeing evil, social injustice, war, poverty, and homelessness as problems rather than as challenges and consequences of our acts, believe that prayer is separation from the "real world" and ask, "What will you do after you rise from prayer?" Some in the church feel that mysticism and spirituality are "spooky" and strange. There are, of course, many ways of praying and many definitions of prayer, from the earliest Christian mystics, who advocated violence and daily mortification to the body, to those who sing and dance and cry with joy or sadness, or work for justice, freedom, and integrating the courage of the prophet with the joy of the mystic. Our definition of prayer reveals our world-view. We can stand on our own two feet, but we cannot stand alone.

Answering Children's Faith Questions Through Parable, Poetry and Prayer was written out of my experience of living with children; their imagination, joy, and questions. Over the years as a teacher of children and of teachers, a parent and a grandparent who is finally comfortable with ambiguity, paradox, and mystery, I became a storyteller and meditator in order to "answer" questions from the heart, as well as the head. Jesus told stories to answer questions. When Jesus was asked a question, he said, "Once upon a time..."

Planting seeds of "sounds in the heart," I have followed Jesus and his parable method. Ever since families have gathered around nomad campfires, and even before, people have been doing so. Today's child, lives in a different setting; high-rise apartment buildings without room to roam, run-down ghettos without sunlight, suburban rows of domino boxes without imagination. In place of stories the television, with all its pros and cons, answers children's questions. Yet in the church and home, school and camp stories are still told that help children find their sense of belonging.

The "facts" we give children today may be obsolete by tomorrow, but the way children learn for themselves, through prayer, parable, and poetry, their imagination and sense of wonder, will last a lifetime.

Answering Children's Faith Questions Through Parable, Poetry and Prayer is a prayerful approach to answering. It is an adventure of being human together, seeing the sacred, the extraordinary in the ordinary, the holiness of all creation, a delightful calling from God, and a commitment to caring. Jesus said, "Go and do likewise."

Suzanne is in her twenties now, and her dad has had years to think about what he might have said that dark night on Canner Street. He might have spoken to her this truth: "Child, it is dark on Canner Street, and the darkness has a power you can almost feel. You will do well to respect it, as you would respect a dangerous tide, but do not fear the darkness. For God surely lives on Canner Street, and has overcome the darkness through the gift of God's own dear child. And you, and I, and every child are protected, armed with God's own protection. So, wear this armor of God, not heavy as Saul's to weigh you down, but God's armor to lift you up. Wear truth about your waist, and the love of God over your heart. Put peace upon your feet. Strap on your arm this shield of faith. Not your own faith, which will doubt and despair and question, but the faithfulness of God. It will turn many darts and arrows. Upon your head wear healing, for Christ shall be your head. And in your hand bear the word of God, and prayer, for this is the gospel truth. Thanks be to God![1] (Paraphrase, Eph 6:10-18)

This resource can be used at home, in a church school class, camp, or worship service setting with children as a way of praying, encouraging and strengthening their relationship with God.

It can also be used to "answer" children's faith questions. The table of contents indicates the theme of each parable. Each one has a guided faith meditation, scripture, poem and a brief prayer to help children learn how to create their own prayer out of their unique relationship with God.

Most children pray by closing their eyes to eliminate distractions. Some children, however, such as those with hearing impairment who need to read the lips of the reader, will pray with open eyes.

Older children can use the book for their own private devotions. If you are the teacher/parent, I urge you to use the material imaginatively, adapting the contents to the age of the child (children) with whom you are working.

Always be open and attentive to any questions that arise before or after using the parable, poetry, and prayer.

*indicates a place to pause in the meditations.

[1]Thanks to Dr. Robert Webber, Lancaster Theological Seminary, Lancaster, PA.Ss

Section A

God

God Is Creator

"In the beginning when God created the heavens and the earth, the earth was a formless void and darkness covered the face of the deep, while a wind from God swept over the face of the waters. Then God said, 'Let there be light'; and there was light." Genesis 1:1-2:3

Sit straight but comfortably in your chair. Place your feet on the floor and your hands in your lap. Close your eyes. Take a deep breath and slowly let it go. Listen to the quiet. You walk into the garden filled with sunlight and butterflies and feel the warmth of the sun on your head, back, arms, body, and legs.* In your imagination, however, it is dark and empty because it is before the beginning of time. Only you and God are there. Then God says, "Let there be light!" The garden is again filled with sunlight as bright as fire. The Voice says, "That is good!"* Then God separates the water from the land, Earth and Seas,* and earth puts forth plants and trees and the Voice says, "That is good!" Then God creates the sun ... and moon ... and stars ... and living creatures. There are red and blue and yellow fish swimming in the river. There are turtles lying on the shore. A white swan glides by, glancing at the deer coming to drink from the river. You walk toward the deer who waits for you to pet it. In this garden no one is afraid.*

A hawk flies overhead and you watch it soar through the sky.* You hear a rustle in the grass and the deer and you look up into the legs, body, neck of a tall giraffe* as a lion dashes out of the woods, lying down at your feet, but you know no one will harm you in this garden.* Then God says, "That is good!" Stay here with the animals for awhile.* Then God creates humankind and blesses them, saying, "That is good!" and the Voice speaks in your direction, "You too are made in my image, blessed." Take time in the silence to enjoy God's presence or ask God a question or thank God for a particular blessing.* When you are ready, knowing you can return to the garden and God's presence whenever you like, return to this room and open your eyes.

"MADE BY HAND"

God pinched
and pounded
and molded the land
from a handful of water
and a bucket of sand.
Then God stuck in His finger
and planted a tree
and the world was created
for you and for me.

Prayer: *Most gracious, loving Creator, we thank You for this beautiful world, for the gift of words and the gift of The Word, Jesus the Christ. Amen.*

God Is Parent

"Then the father said to him 'Son, you are always with me, and all that is mine is yours. But we had to celebrate and rejoice, because this brother of yours was dead and has come to life; he was lost and has been found.'" Luke 15:11-32

In your faith imagination you come into the sanctuary of the church. It is Sunday morning and you are attending a worship service at church with your family. You are sitting in the pew between your mother and father and the minister says, "Will the children come to the altar for children's time?" You stand up and walk to the front of the church and sit on the steps. The minister says, "I am going to tell you a story about a loving father: Once upon a time there was a man who had two sons. The younger of them said to his father, 'Father, give me my share of my inheritance now.' That was against the law of the people. The giving of the inheritance, while the father was still alive, was the breaking of the relationship, the separation of the father and the son. Yet because the father loved his son, he gave, and the son left. He traveled to a distant country, and there he spent, wasted all he had, and found himself without money or friends. He fed the pigs, and would willingly have eaten their food, but no one gave him anything. When he came to himself he said, "I will go to my father and tell

17

him I am sorry. I am no longer worthy to be called his son."
While he was coming home, still far off, his father saw his lost
child and was filled with love and compassion. He ran to him
and put his arms around him and kissed him." The minister
smiles at you and says, "This is the story Jesus told, saying,
God is like that father. God's love covers all." You return to the
pew where you were sitting with your loving parents.

GOD'S PATIENCE — John 3:16

God, You must be very patient
And very, very kind,
And very understanding
To constantly remind
Us, people of Your promise,
"With Me you will be one."
You told us through the prophets
Who showed what You had done.
You even wrote a letter
Addressed to everyone,
But, still we would not listen,
And so You sent Your Son.

Prayer: Dear God, we thank You for Your promise, for the
Bible, and for Your Son. Help us become Your
loving children. In Christ's name. Amen.

God Is The Smile In Our Lives

"Peace be to the whole community, and love with faith, from God the Father and the Lord Jesus Christ." Ephesians 6:23

In your faith imagination go back to a time before you were born when African Americans had separate schools, could not drink out of the water fountains white people used, and had to sit in the back of buses. Now you are in front of a school and the first African American is walking toward the school to enter. The people have angry looks on their faces and cruel words in their mouths. They shout, "Go home, nigger. This school is for whites only!" You see a young African American slowly walk toward the strange school. She had never been there before. It was a school "for whites only." She recalled her father's words, "Leslie, are you sure you want to do this?" "God told me to," she had replied. She saw Father glance over his shoulder at Mother and then he turned back to Leslie and said, "Then, Leslie, God be with you." As you stand among the crowd, how do you feel? What do you think?* As Leslie listens to the segregationists scream curses at her, she looks around, suddenly afraid. She is alone. One black girl in a mob of angry whites.* You see her stop. She closes her eyes to ask God for courage and love, hearing her father's words, "God be with you," and suddenly Leslie sees God smiling. Leslie opens her eyes and smiles, and continues walking toward the school that once-upon-a-time was "for whites only."

GOD LOVES US

See the lovely lilies,
How beautiful they grow
From the rain and sunshine,
How they help us know
God's love for God's creation,
Each bird, each flower, each tree,
And Jesus said, "Even more than these,
God loves you and me."

Prayer: *Dear God, You are the smile in our lives. We thank You for Your love and guidance and for the beauty of Your creation of people and flowers of many different sizes and shapes and colors. Amen.*

God Is Love

"Whoever does not love does not know God,
for God is love."   *1 John 4:8*

In your faith imagination you are a new boy or girl at school and it is hard for you to make new friends. You miss your best friend and wish you had not had to move. Suddenly someone speaks to you, a child your age, "Are you new here?" You reply, "Yes," and share names. "Have you made any friends here yet?" You shake your head number "Would you like to come over to my house after school this afternoon?" You hesitate, wondering if you should take the risk. Then you answer, "I'll call my Mom."

After spending the afternoon with your new friend, when you arrive home for dinner that evening, you tell your folks all about your new friend. Mother says, "I'm glad you found a friend. I need one, too. What is your friend's mother like?" "She was nice because she gave us milk and cookies to eat."

That night in your prayer you thank God for all the people who love you, showing you God's love and all the gifts God gives you out of that love. Name those gifts now, thanking God, and when you are ready, return to this place and open your eyes."

GOD'S CARE

No dress nor suit of clothes will ever be
As lovely as the leaves upon a tree,
As flowers that neither weave nor spin,
And yet are robed more beautiful than royal men.
If God plans for flowers in their finery,
Think how much more God cares for you and me!

Prayer: Dear God, thank You, for the "cookies and milk" that show people love and care for us and love You, because You first loved us. Amen.

Where Is God?

"For the Lord is a sun and shield..."
Psalm 84:11

In your faith imagination you are at the airport, waiting to board the airplane and soar among the white fluffy clouds. Today, however, the airport is dark and gloomy. There are only gray clouds and it is raining. "Where is the sun?" you wonder and wish you could see it.* Mother is seated beside you so you ask her aloud, "Where is the sun? I wish I could see it." Mother closes her book and says, "It is there even though you cannot see it." You reply "All these gray days make me feel sad, alone, and cold." Mother smiles as she says again, "The sun is there even when you cannot see it." * At last you hear them call your flight number and you walk toward the plane and find your seat and sit down and strap on your seatbelt. Suddenly you are above the clouds. The sun is shining and you shout, "It is there even though I couldn't see it!" Then you are quiet...thinking, "This must be what they mean about God. Although I do not see or hear or touch God, God is here, like the sun." Now return to this place and remember that God is with you everywhere.

WHEREVER GOD IS

I used to wonder,
When I was seven,
Where is the place
Adults call "heaven"?
But I've discovered
Now that I'm eleven,
Wherever God is,
That is heaven.

Prayer: *Dear God in heaven and on earth, thank You for life and learning and being with me to guide and comfort me wherever I am. Amen.*

God Plans For Food, Flowers, And Faith

"Therefore I tell you, do not worry about your life, what you will eat or what you will drink, or about your body, what you will wear. Is not life more than food...?"   *Matt. 6:25-33*

In your faith imagination you are at church camp. Because you have been late to lunch three days in a row, when you arrive at lunch that day, your counselor says, "I'm sorry, but it's too late for lunch. All the food has been served." You are disappointed, of course, but cannot let the others see that it matters to you. "I'm not hungry anyway," you mumble, as you walk away. That had been an hour ago. You weren't hungry then, but now your stomach grumbles and groans aloud. "Oh, hush!" you grumble back. The swimming and hiking had been fun that morning, but now you know that all that fun has made you even more hungry. And if that wasn't enough, you were half asleep at breakfast and had picked at your eggs and pushed away your toast and milk. You sit down on the ground and lean against a tree, and without thinking pull up a small, yellow dandelion. "You're lucky," you say to the small flower. "I'll bet you never get hungry." You close your eyes. The whole world seems to be resting under the heat of the sun and the dandelion seems to speak to you saying, "I get hungry too. I am fed by the soil in which I live, the rain and the sun. If there were no sun or water, there would be no food, no life on earth. It takes a Plan to create air and water and sunlight that will mix inside green plants to make food." "If there is a Plan, there must be a Planner!" you explode with this, and open your eyes.

"There you are!" the counselor said, seeing you with the dandelion resting on your stomach. "You must be hungry, if you are hungry enough to eat a dandelion!" You smile. "It's the best food in the good world," "Is it as good as a peanut butter sandwich?" your counselor asked, handing you a gooey peanut butter sandwich, covered with sweet, purple jelly. You smile again, without answering, for your mouth is full of gooey peanut better and jelly. Now return to this place.

LOOK AT THE LILIES

Look at the lilies of the field,
They toil not, neither spin
And still we spend our days
In anxious worries how to win
A sense of meaning in our lives,
The gift God simply gives
To those who in the company
Of faith and flowers lives.

Prayer: *We thank You, Creator God, for Your plan for beauty, and flowers, for good food to eat, and for faith, which is the meaning of our lives. Amen.*

God Is With Us

*"And those who know your name put their trust
in you, for you, O Lord, have not forsaken those who
seek you."*   *Psalm 9:10*

In your faith imagination it is Father's Day. The minister gathers the children around him at the altar. One of them is his own three-year-old son. Every Sunday the children gather to hear stories. Some from the Bible, and some about themselves. They like sitting on the altar steps, close to their pastor friend. Now he looks into their eyes and smiles, for he loves the children. Because it is Father's Day, he asks them, "What do you like best about your daddy?" Alan says, "My daddy's big!" Alice says, "My daddy fixes things." "I like my daddy's prickly chin before he shaves," says Lucy. "He's funny and he's fun," adds Philip. Each child names one thing they like about their father. When all of the children have spoken, the pastor looks at his own son. "Michael, what do you like best?" Michael smiles at his father, who was a very busy man. Then he replies, "When he's with me!" Then the minister turns to you and asks you, "What do you like best about your father?" If you wish you may substitute another person who loves you. You reply and think about how God is with you. When you are ready, return to this place.

PRAISE THE LORD

The heavens are glad,
The skies are full,
And every floating cloud
And flying bird sings aloud
To praise the Lord.

The earth rejoices,
The land gives birth,
And every bursting seed
 And blooming flower sings
To praise the Lord.

The sea roars,
The waters leap,
And every sandy shore
And swimming fish joyfully adore
And praise the Lord.

The fields exalt,
The lambs grow fat,

And every creeping thing
And growing grain begin
   to sing
To praise the Lord.

The trees blossom
And shout for joy,
And every bud
And greening leaf above
Sing songs of love
To praise the Lord.

Prayer: Dear Lord, with all creation we praise You and thank You for Your presence among and within us. In Christ Jesus' name. Amen.

God Is The One Who Is With Us

"He (God) said, 'I will be with you.'" Ex. 3:12a

In your faith imagination you are in the woods at night observing a young Native American boy. You watch and listen. "Alone?" the boy asked. He was brave but... "Did you say I was to stay in the forest one night <u>alone</u>?" His father replied, "You have passed the tests of the tribe for speed. How fast you ran! I was proud of you, my son. You showed us you know how to hunt and fight. Now this is your last trail before the tribe considers you a man, the most difficult of all. You are to spend one night alone in the forest until I come for you in the morning." The boy was led into the deepest, darkest part of the forest and left there alone. At first he was not afraid but the longer he stayed in the woods, the more frightening the dark became, the louder the sounds of the night. He saw things that moved coming closer and closer toward him. The boy ran from them. He ran and ran. Then he remembered that this was a test of his courage. Others had done it before him. He was about to become a man, responsible for himself. A man does not run but faces the dark. He returned to the place he had been left and stayed there all night. When dawn came the following morning, he was surprised to hear, "Good morning." Looking up he saw his father standing behind the nearest tree. "How did it go, son?" he asked. The boy replied, "It is good to see you. The dark can be frightening, but I am glad for what it taught me. Being alone is scarey." "You were not alone, my son. I was with you through the night." "If I had known that," the boy-become-man said, "I would have slept more soundly through the night!" You are glad the boy passed the test in the dark and remember that God has promised to be with us in the light and in the dark. When you are ready, return to this place.

AND IT WAS GOOD

In the beginning it was dark, as dark as night.
And God said, "Let there be light!"
And there was light, the sun and moon and stars so bright.
And it was good.
Then God said, "Let there be land, and let there be sea."
And God created fish and seeds and apple tree.
And from the seeds God created food, and it was good.
Then God made the animals; the snake, the cow.
And when God finished, God said, "Now
Let us make man and woman, too,"
And all was fresh and bright and new.
And it was good!

Prayer: *Dear God, we love You as the One who is with us so we know we are not alone and sleep more soundly through the night. Amen.*

Where Is God's Dwelling?

*"God is love, and those who abide in love
abide in God, and God abides in them."*

1 John 4:16b

In your faith imagination you are sitting in your church school class when the teacher asks you and the other students, "Where is the dwelling of God?" You all look at her and each other and then you stand up and smile, stretching your arms as far as you are able and say, "All of creation is the place where God dwells." Then the teacher, as if she had not heard, answers her own questions: "God's dwelling is wherever we let God come in." When you are ready, return to this place.

THE KINGDOM OF LOVE

Imagine the power
Of a loving God
Who knows our every need,
Who can cause a tall
And a mighty tree
To grow from a tiny seed!

Think of beginning
A kingdom of love,
As tiny as a grain,
That will grow and grow
'Til the world is one
Where God will always reign.

Prayer: *Dear God, we thank You for Your creation, Your church, and wherever You live among and within us. Amen.*

What Is Heaven?

"The Lord's throne is in heaven."   Psalm 11:4

In your faith imagination you are in your church school class, talking about God and Moses and the story of the burning bush, when God spoke to Moses in the bush that did not burn. Someone asks, "Why, of all things, did God choose a humble bush as the place from which to speak with Moses?" Everyone is silent, waiting. You wonder what the pastor will answer because you know he prefers to ask questions than to answer them. His answers are usually a story. You sit back with the others and wait.* Your pastor replies: " If God had chosen the mighty tree of Lebanon or the Empire State Building, we would ask the same question. Why do you think God chose the bush from which to speak with Moses?" Still we wait, but now we begin to think. "Why?" Then the pastor answers his own question. "God chose the humble thornbush to teach us that there is no place on earth without the Divine Presence, not even a thornbush." You think about God's presence here and now with you and thank God for God's love,* and when you are ready, return to this place and open your eyes.

HEAVEN IS ...

Heaven is higher than higher than
   higher,
Heaven is higher than I can see.
Heaven is bigger than bigger than
   bigger,
And in the beginning, surrounded by
   sea.
Heaven is bluer than bluer than bluer,
As long as I've known it, the heaven's
   been blue.
Heaven's been always, forever and
   ever,
Without a beginning or ending, as You.

Prayer: *Dear God, You and heaven are wonderful mysteries. Thank You for Your presence in our lives. Help me learn that it is better to give praise and thanks than to understand all mysteries. We pray in the name of Christ our Lord. Amen.*

What Does The Lord Require?

"He has told you, O mortal, what is good; and what does the Lord require of you but to do justice, and to love kindness, and to walk humbly with your God?" Micah 6:8

In your faith imagination you go back to the time when the prophet Micah lived. You enter the crowded village street and listen. "Everyone is taking bribes, Micah. If we don't, someone else will." Micah shook his head. "It is a sin against God..." "Don't play goody-goody with us, Micah. We are taking the money," the men replied. Micah had heard of bribery in high places but he did not believe God's people would forget their Law. * "If this is true, perhaps the other things I have heard are also true," Micah said aloud, as he walked through the dirty streets of Samaria, littered with garbage and refuse. With Micah you see a dirty beggar pick up a piece of food from the filthy street and greedily eat it. Micah suddenly notices you and says, "The people are starving, while those in high places cheat and steal, ignoring the needs of the poor."

As you enter the marketplace you see a poor beggar. "Your son for a pair of shoes! " says the merchant, rubbing his hands to keep them warm. "Hurry up. Make up your mind. It is cold out here." The old man holds the hand of a small boy.

Neither of them is wearing shoes, their feet purple from the cold, bleeding as well, from the hard cobblestones. "But he is my son. Give me the shoes and I will be able to work and pay you double," the poor man begs. "Get out of here until you can return with something more than a worthless promise for a pair of good shoes!" shouts the merchant. "I have always kept my promise. I may be poor but I am truthful." The old man falls on his knees before the merchant. "Be kind and God will bless you." "As God has blessed you?" mocks the merchant. The old man begins to cry. The merchant raises his arm, as if to strike the poor beggar and Micah, unable to stand it no longer runs toward the merchant, grabbing his arm. "You have no right to strike." "The poor have no rights..." growled the merchant, interrupting Micah. "Who do you think you are?" Micah ignores the merchant's question and asks, "How much are the shoes?" The merchant begins to laugh until he remembers that a sale is involved. He can laugh after he has his money! Micah pays the merchant the price he asked and gave the old man the shoes. "Come with me," he says. You follow behind, watching.* When the old man and his son have eaten, Micah gives them a few coins. "Go in peace and God bless you." "God bless you. Master." Suddenly you notice that you are passing the synagogue. You see the people in their fine clothes praying and offering their tithes to God. "I came to the city to pray but my heart is too sad," Micah says to you as he glances again at the congregation gathered, unaware of the sick and lonely, the poor people outside.* "He has showed you, O man, what is good; and what does the Lord require of you?" Micah was thinking of his friends' greed for money, of the hungry beggars in the street, eating food from the gutters, of the poor, sick, and shoeless old and young people and the satisfied people in the sanctuary. Micah shook his head. "What does the Lord require of you?" he asked again.* You do not know what to answer when Micah continues, answering his own question: "But to do justice, and to love kindness, and to walk humbly with your God." Then Micah turns and walks out of the city gates to his home. You follow him up the dusty highway and watch him, knowing that he will never forget that day in the city and for the rest of his life, he will work for and preach justice for all people, rich and poor, young and old, wise and unlearned, because he walks humbly with his Lord.* When you are ready, knowing that you can return to Micah and his story, open your eyes and be in this place.

GOD'S LOVE

I'd like to paint a picture of God for you
With sparkling stars and glistening dew,
Silver threads of snails' trails and spider webs.
I'd like to tell a tale to help you see God
In all God's colors, sounds, and tastes.
But especially I'd like for you
To feel God's love and presence everywhere,
But that is something only God can do.
And all that's left for me is loving you.

Prayer: *God, help me remember the story of Micah, his question and his answer, knowing Your presence and love at all times. Amen.*

The Lord Is My Shepherd

"The Lord is my shepherd."   *Psalm 23:1*

The psalmist lived among sheep and shepherds and sang, "The Lord is my shepherd." In your faith imagination picture the different ways you think of God. You know how much God cares for you, what do you love most? Think about those in your family who mean the most to you and care for you. God loves you even more! Reflect on these things, remembering that prayer is your relationship with God. When you are ready, open your eyes and return to this place.

ONE HUNDRED SHEEP

One hundred sheep
Not one the same!
And yet the shepherd knew them
Name by name by name.
He knew when one
Of them was gone
And searched and searched for him

From night to dawn.
He searched until
At last he found the sheep
And all of them were safe
Within his keep.
And Jesus said,
"God cares for you,
For God is like
A shepherd, too."

Prayer: *Thank you, God, for Your love and care in creation, in Christ, in the people who love and care for us. Amen.*

The Still, Small Voice

"Be still and know that I am God."
I Kings 19:12

invite you to place your feet flat on the floor, your hands in your lap, to close your eyes and take a deep breath, breathing in God's silence and breathing out your need to control your thoughts, feelings, or images. Feel the silence wrap you as a blanket of love. In this silence you feel a great longing for God. The word of the Lord says, "Go out and stand on the mountain before the Lord, for the Lord is about to pass by." You go and stand on the mountain. * Suddenly there is a great wind., so strong that it splits the mountains and breaks the rocks in pieces, but the Lord is not in the wind. Feel the great wind of some strong struggle you are experiencing at present. * And after the wind an earthquake, but the Lord is not in the earthquake.* And after the earthquake a fire, but the Lord was not in the fire. After the fire there is no sound—sheer silence. In the silence God puts out the fire and you encounter God. Speak with God or sit in silence in the peace of God's presence.* And when you are ready return to this place and open your eyes.

WHEN THE WIND BLOWS

When the wind blows, leaves fly and
    bend,
Though I have never seen the wind.
When people love and show they care,
Though I can't see God, I know God's
    there.[1]

*Prayer: Dear Lord, thank You for silence in which we can
hear you speak and for Your love that helps us to
love and care. Amen.*

[1] Elaine M, Ward, <u>Love in a Lunchbox</u> (Nashville, TN: Abingdon), 1996, p. 92.

Section B

Jesus

Jesus Loves And Welcomes Us

" 'Let the little children come to me; do not stop them; for it is to such as these that the kingdom of God belongs.' "

Mark 10:13-16

Center by closing your eyes, placing your feet flat on the floor, sitting erect, hands in lap, and take three slow, deep breaths. Now imagine yourself on the seashore. Feel the warm sun on your back and neck and arms. Smell the sea. Listen to the seagulls. Be aware that Jesus is there.* You see Jesus telling a group of people stories about God's love and promise. You approach and listen.* Suddenly there is a disturbance in the crowd. A loud voice is rebuking a child. Everyone is silent, and Jesus says softly, "Let the children come to me." He places them on his lap and blesses them. Then the children run off, happily, to play, but you stay.* Jesus looks at you. Look into his eyes now, as he motions for you to come closer. You do.* Jesus smiles and asks, "How may I help you?" You tell him your honest thoughts, questions, and feelings.* Let Jesus respond and listen carefully.* Do what you must do and when you are ready, return to this place and open your eyes.

WELCOME

> So welcome was the little room,
> So full of joy and care,
> Of wonder and of happiness,
> I knew God's love was there.

Prayer: *Dear God, thank You for my church school room, for Jesus' welcoming children, and for Your love. Amen.*

Jesus Is Like A Good Shepherd

"I am the good shepherd. The good shepherd lays down his life for the sheep."   John 10:11

In your faith imagination you are in a church school class. Your teacher is telling you the story Jesus told of the Good Shepherd who had one hundred sheep for whom he loved and cared. One day one of the sheep wandered away. The good shepherd searched and searched for the one lost lamb until he found it, and returning to the others, he rejoiced. They had a party and celebrated. Then your teacher says, "Let's pretend we are the lost sheep." Everyone scrambled onto the floor on their knees, pretending to be sheep and each lamb escaped into a corner. The teacher as a good shepherd worried about the children getting lost or hurt, but no sooner rescued one lost lamb, than another one escaped, and she had to rescue that one, until at one point there were more lost sheep than there were in the fold.* As one of the sheep, you enjoy the play as you hear one of the teachers say, "Perhaps the sheep need a good feeding trough in the sheepfold," and quickly called everyone to, snack time. Everyone comes to the table for cookies and juice. Then it is time for church. After church, driving home your father asks,

"What did you learn in Sunday School today?" You tell him the story of the good shepherd. "And what did you learn from that story?" your father asks.* Think now what you might answer.* Then return to this place.

INASMUCH—Matthew 25:40

If I had lived when Jesus lived, I'd ask him in to tea
And give him gifts and listen to the stories he told me.
He never would be lonely and he never would be cold,
For I would keep him company, and then when I was old,
I'd bring my children unto him. But Jesus said, "You see,
Inasmuch as you love others, you show your love for me."

Prayer: Dear Good Shepherd, thank You for Your love. Help me show that love to others. Amen.

The Shared Christmas Gift

"So they went with haste and found Mary and Joseph, and the child lying in the manger."
Luke 2:16

In your faith imagination it is a time before Christmas. You are in your class at church school when the teacher says, "Some children will have no Christmas this year, so our church school is asking each of you to bring a new or used gift to give. We give gifts at Christmas to celebrate God's gift of love, Jesus, at Christmas." Even the television showed children, saying, "These children need your love and support." So when Mother said, "Today is the day we go Christmas shopping," you think about the children and what you have seen and heard. This Christmas you are especially excited about Christmas shopping because you have been saving all year to buy your mother a special Christmas gift, because last year Mother spent Christmas in the hospital. This year is special because Mother is home and all the family will be together. You quickly finish breakfast, brush your teeth, comb your hair, and dress. It is the long-awaited day! The streets downtown are busy. The sidewalks are crowded. Among the noise of commotion there is a spirit of joy and excitement. The ringing of bells adds to the merriment. You watch the bells being rung by a woman in a black hat and black dress before you ask your mother, "Who is she?

Why is she ringing bells?" Mother replies, "The bells are the sounds of Christmas, along with the angels singing, the shepherds shouting as they ran to the manger, the wise men humming as they brought their gifts to the newborn king." The bells were the background to Mother's story. You listen to them both. "The people ringing the bells are calling to us to ask for our coins to share food and clothing and gifts this Christmas," Mother continued. You remember again the sad children's faces on the television and the words of your teachers at school and church. Then just before Mother can open her purse, she hears the "ping" in the pot and your cry, "Oh, no, I just gave the money I had saved for the Christmas gift I was going to buy you." You are surprised and now sad at what you have done crying, "I'm so sorry!" Mother smiles. "It is the best Christmas gift you could give me. It is a Christmas gift we can share together."

THE GIFT OF LOVE

The gift of love begins in the heart,
In the thought of the one who cares,
In the time that it takes to think and plan
For the love that the giver shares.
The gift of love is a simple gift,
No matter how large or how small,
For the giver offering himself
Is the greatest gift of all.

Prayer: *Dear God, Father of our Lord Jesus Christ, we praise Your name at Christmas and thank You for the gift of Your eternal love. In Christ's name. Amen.*

The Angels' Notes

"In the wilderness prepare the way of the LORD, make straight in the desert a highway for our God."   Isaiah 40:3

In your faith imagination on December the first you see on the wall opposite the front door a large wall hanging of twenty-four angels with great white wings. On one of the pair of wings is written a number from one to twenty-four and pinned to each hand a note. Each day you are allowed to open that day's note and read it aloud. The notes begin "In the wilderness prepare the way of the LORD, make straight in the desert a highway for our God" (Isaiah 40:3) "... And they went with haste and found Mary and Joseph, and the child lying in a manger" (Luke 2:16). The notes not only told the sacred story but each day led to small gifts of books, cookies, and socks. The day you read the note from Psalm 149: "Let them praise God's name with dancing," the whole family went to the water park to watch the dolphins dance. Each day was a surprise, but the last note holds the best surprise, the greatest gift of all. It is the only note that every year is different. You wonder what it will say this year. At last it is Christmas Eve. You take the note from the angel's hand and slowly read, "They went with haste..." "Come!" your father interrupts, opening the door, as together you stare at the sky-filled night. Never before had the stars seemed so alive, so full of fire and energy, "Wow!" you whisper into the darkness, sitting down on the blanket your father has spread on the ground. It is so still it feels like the beginning of time. Father reads from the Bible: "In the beginning..." Life! Here they were together, alive! "...And they saw the child lying in a manger," God's love in a human form, "...And it was good" says the Bible. When you are ready to leave, return to this place.

ONCE UPON A CHRISTMAS EVE

Once upon a Christmas Eve angels sang with joy,
Telling shepherds in the field of the baby boy
Who was born in Bethlehem in a stable where
Cows and sheep surrounded him in a manger there.
Mary with her lullaby, Joseph with his song,
Sang their praises to the Lord all night long,
'Til the coming of that day, that first Christmas Morn,
When Jesus, promise of God's hope and love,
Named "Mighty God," was born.

Prayer: *Glory be to You, 0 God, in this special time of Advent for that first Christmas Morn, when Your promise of love was born. "And it was good." Amen and Amen!*

After Advent: Jesus And The Rich Man

"Sell all that you have and give it to the poor and you will have riches in heaven. Then come and follow me."

Luke 18:18-30

In your faith imagination you are in the land where Jesus lived. A man in rich, thick velvet robes, with brilliant rings on his fingers, rides up to Jesus. When he dismounts from his horse, he comes to Jesus to ask how he can be saved. Jesus tells him, and he says he has done all that. Jesus looks at him with love and says, "You need to do one more thing. Sell all that you have and give it to the poor and you will have riches in heaven. Then come and follow me." * You see the man become sad, mount his horse, and go away sorrowing. Jesus' disciples ask, "Who then can be saved?" Jesus replies, "With God all things are possible." * You think about how you are like the rich man until he comes again into your imagination. This time he is old, and you enter into his home where he is sitting, surrounded by thick oriental carpets, pearl-inlaid furniture, heavy brocaded curtains and rich foods, but he is not happy. He is thinking about the day he went to the wandering preacher, the one some said was "the Son of God," and asked him how he could inherit eternal life.* Jesus' reply had been too demanding, too unreasonable. What did this poor preacher know about money? The old man remembers the great sorrow he had felt as he left Jesus. Today he is even richer than he was then, long ago, and in this mood he falls asleep.* In his dream he again encounters Jesus. Once more Jesus looks at him with love. "Have you used God's gifts well?" Jesus asks. "I have tithed. I have given one-tenth of my riches to charity," the old man replies. "You have given what was not yours." "No! No! I have only given what belonged to me. I have never taken from anyone," he protests.* "What you have belongs to them. Is it better to have wealth or to give it away? Sell all that you have and give it to the poor and then come and follow me." The words are the same ones Jesus spoke to him long ago. Was he being given a second chance?* "But, Master, I am too old to follow you now." Again the man is full of sorrow. It is too late. If only he had listened to Jesus the first time! The old man begins to cry. If only it were possible to have a second chance! "With God all things are possible," Jesus says. * You watch the old man awake from his sleep. He looks at his thick rich carpets, his expensive curtains, his priceless furniture and slowly lifts himself to his feet. As you follow him, selling all that he has and giving it to the poor, you see him smile, a "richer" man than he had ever been before. Now he was surrounded by God.* What you have seen invites you to pray and you do so now.* When you have expressed your thoughts and feelings to God in prayer, return to this place and open your eyes.

AFTER ADVENT

Dear Lord, when the song of the angels
is still
And the candles of Advent are out,
When wild winter returns with its chill
And faith is frozen in doubt,
Then let the message of Christmas
begin again . . .
> Peace to all nations
> Good news to the poor,
> Power to the weak,
> Food for the hungry,
> Sight for the blind,
> Hope for the meek,
> Fire for the altar of love within.
> Amen.

Prayer: *God, for whom all things are possible, open my eyes to Your love, giving me a "second chance" through the promise of Your son, our Lord, Jesus Christ. Amen.*

Section C

The Earth

Taking Care Of The World

"They shall not hurt nor destroy on all my holy mountain; for the earth shall be full of the knowledge of the Lord, as the waters cover the sea." Is. 11:9

In your faith imagination enter the "once-upon-a-time" land and the imagination of Dr. Seuss. It is a strange land. You see a Once-ler on his Whisper-ma-Phone and hear him telling of the days way back when the grass was still green and the pond was still wet and the clouds were still clean and there were Truffula Trees! Out of the Truffula Trees, the Once-ler knitted a Thneed by chopping down a Truffula Tree. They became so popular that, crazy with greed, he called all of his relatives. They built a factory and began chopping down Truffula Trees until the Lorax, arising out of one of the stumps, spoke for the trees who had no tongues and the animals who were starving because they had no food.* You wonder what the Once-ler will do and see him, though feeling sad, send them away, for business is business. Bigger and bigger grew the factory, the roads, the wagons, the loads, and the Lorax returned to complain of the smoke and the smog in the Swomee-Swans' throat. Soon there was only one solution: they must leave. They left the leftover goo from the machinery that chugged on day and night without stopping and the

Once-ler continued getting bigger and BIGGER. And all that was left was a small pile of rocks, with the one word ... UNLESS.* As you watch, you become very angry and sad, and the Once-ler says, "Unless someone like you cares a whole awful lot, nothing is going to get better. It's not."* And you reply, "To plant, treat the earth with care, give it clean water, feed it fresh air, grow a forest, protect it from axes that hack, so the Lorax and all of his friends may come back."[1]* Knowing you too may come back, you return to this room and open your eyes.

UNLESS

Once the eagle, crane, all birds were proud and free,
Soaring high above the earth, the sea.
Now the air is filled with smog instead of birds,
"O beautiful for spacious skies ..." forgotten words.
Seas are poisoned by our waste, earth by our mess.
Someday earth and sea may be no more...
Unless...

Prayer: Dear Father, hear and bless
Thy beasts and singing birds:
And guard with tenderness
Small things that have no words.

— Unknown

[1] Dr. Seuss. The Lorax (New York: Random House, 1971).

The World (And The Well) Belong To All

"Have we not all one father?"   Malachi 2:10

In your faith imagination travel to Haiti where once upon a time there was a drought when the wells and streams dried up and the animals decided to ask God for help. As you enter this land of enchantment where even the animals talk, you hear God promise, "I will give you one well for everyone to use," when God heard their problem. "One of you will have to stay with the well and make sure it stays clean." The lizard volunteered and God appointed him the watchman of the well. You watch as one by one the animals come to the well to drink. They are very thirsty, but you hear the lizard ask in a deep voice, "Who is walking in my grove?" The cow replies, "It is I, the cow, coming for water." "Go away. The well is dry," says the lizard. The cow goes away and suffered from thirst, as the horse comes. "Who is walking in my grove?" asks the lizard. "It is I, the horse, coming for water." "Go away. The well is dry." You watch the horse go away, suffering from thirst. As each animal comes to the well, you hear the lizard tell them the same thing. So at last God comes to the well. "Who is walking in my grove," asked the lizard. "It is I, Papa God, come for water." "Go away, Papa God. The well is dry." You do not believe what you are hearing, but God sends for the animals to come to the well. God speaks: "If a man has a banana or a pineapple or a mango tree in his garden, it is his, but if a man has a well in his garden, the hole in the ground is his, but the water is God's. From now on the lizard will drink his water from puddles when it rains and the frog will be the new caretaker." And the animals drink at the well and all night, each night, the frog cries out, "This is God's well." Remembering that God gives us everything we need, return to this place.

THE HOUSE OF THE WORLD

The house of the world has a roof made of sky
With space in the attic for clouds to pass by.
Each room in the house has windows for light,
So the stars and the moon may be seen in the night.
There's a mat that says, "Welcome" that stands by the
    door,
And bright blooming flowers cover the floor.
The kitchen is warmed from the heart of the sun.
It's the house of the Lord, built for everyone.

> **Prayer:** *Dear Creator God, we thank You for wells and water and the world that we all share together. Help us remember that the sun and sea and sky are Yours. Amen.*

The Earth Is The Lord's

"The earth is the Lord's and all that is in it..."
Psalm 24:1

Ask the children to center *(feet on floor, hands in lap, back straight, eyes closed, breathe deeply)*. In your faith imagination it is almost dark. We walk together into the woods. The birds are singing their good-night songs, the crickets are chirping good-bye. The bright red sun fills the sky as it says farewell.* You smell the trees, see the squirrels chasing one another from branch to branch. A rabbit watches us warily, nibbling a carrot. A deer comes to the pond beside our path. There is peace and harmony here in the woods.* Knowing God has created the world for all creatures and that it is good, suddenly you are filled with love for God's world* and thank God, promising to take care of it. We sit down together on the path, thinking of a way we can help God care for the world.* When you are ready, return to this place and open your eyes.

WITH WONDER

A child with wonder reaches out for life,
As growing flowers reaching toward the
light.
The sense of wonder is our search for
God,
Who plans this wondrous world that
gives delight.

Prayer: Dear God, thank You for creation in which we are
one with birds and animals and all people. Open
our eyes and ears to the wonders around us. In
Christ's name we pray. Amen.

What I Can Do

"The child grew..."   Luke 2:40

In your faith imagination you are seated at the table with your family. Father says, "Please close the door." You get up and go the door but it is heavy. You push and push and push. Everyone sits at the table waiting. You try again to push against the heavy door, but it will not move. The wind is blowing from the other side of the door while you push from the opposite. Over and over you try to shut the door, as you have been asked to do. No one at the table says, "I'll help you." They know you can do it. No one at the table gets up to help you, because you want to do it yourself. No one at the table says, "Hurry, the food is getting cold," for they know you can do it. At last, putting your shoulder against the door and pushing your very hardest, the door closes with a bang. You return to the table and smile. Everyone sitting at the table returns your smile to thank you for your help.

Whenever you feel or think, "I can't," remember the famous baseball player, Babe Ruth who hit 714 home runs, but also struck out 1330 times! Going up to bat means sometimes going down, swinging. It didn't stop Babe Ruth. It need not stop you! Think of three things you'd like to be able to do, and then open your eyes and return to this place.

HELP ME TO SEE

"I've praised and I've answered,
I've comforted you.
I've shown you my love, child,
What more can I do?"

"I'd like you to listen,
To help me to see
The blueprint that God
Drew especially for me,
To help me discover,
To seek and to know
The gifts that I have,
To coax them to grow.
If you'll only listen,
I'll find the design,
And work out the pattern
God made to be mine."

Prayer: *Dear God, help me have the courage to try again whenever I feel discouraged or afraid. Amen.*

Section D

Other
Faith
Questions

What Is Imagination?

"All were amazed and perplexed, saying to one another, 'What does this mean?'"   Acts 2:12

In your faith imagination you are riding on a white cloud watching God with great imagination, imagining a person, breathing into the person God's living breath. Then God places the person and some others on the arc of the rainbow beside you, and God gives a gentle push to the people and they slide down the side of the rainbow until they touch the Earth. Your cloud floats lower and you watch the people stand up and look around. When they realize they are alone, they shiver and wrap their arms around themselves, for they are cold, alone and fearful. They look up into heaven, longing to return to God. They try to climb the rainbow but it is steep and slippery and there are no handrails. The people suddenly sit down on the ground, and feeling helpless and hopeless, they cry. It is sad to watch them feel so alone. You want to speak but instead God sees the fear and loneliness, the sadness and longing, and God wraps a gift for them and grabs a cloud to send it flying down the rainbow, landing on top of the people. Unwrapping the gift from God, they hug it to their hearts and smile, for they are no longer lonely nor sad. The gift of God is faith imagination in which we know the presence of

God-with-us, the Holy Spirit of God within us. Knowing that you too have received this gift of God, you return to this place and open your eyes.

IMAGINATION IS...

"Imagination is the beginning of creation,
You imagine what you desire;
You will what you imagine;
And at last you create what you will."
— *Padraic Colum*

Prayer: *Thank You, God, for faith imagination in which we experience Your presence and love. Help me to keep it alive through prayer. Amen.*

The Answer Is In Your Hands

"Great is the LORD and greatly to be praised..."

Psalm 48:1

Close your eyes. Jesus is leading you into your center where the Spirit of God dwells. In your faith imagination you sit down on the grass and begin to ask Jesus all kinds of questions, "Where is God? What does God took like? Does God answer prayers? Why didn't God answer my prayer?" Jesus is silent. Then he smiles and says, "Let me tell you a story. Long ago and yesterday when stories roamed the earth, a king heard of a wise man, a teacher. The king invited him to his home. 'I have heard much about you', he said to the wise man, 'for they say you are a learned man. They say you have powers of transformation, that you can read and heal peoples' minds. I too am a man of learning and would like you to prove to me your powers. In my hands behind my back is a bird. Is it alive or is it dead?' The sage, the wise man, was silent. The sage could not speak because he was afraid that as the result of what he said, he could kill the bird if the bird were still alive. So he did not speak. The king looked at the sage and smiled and the sage looked into the eyes of the king and was silent. The king waited. The silence hung heavy as a sword over the head of the sage and then he said, 'Your majesty, the answer is in your hands.'"* Now Jesus is silent. Then he smiles at you and asks, "Does that answer your question?" Together you sit in silence, thinking about what the story says to you.* Then Jesus repeats, "The answer is in your hands and in your heart and faith imagination." Open your eyes and return to this place.

ALL THAT GOD DOES IS DONE WELL

A rabbi went out into the dark, dark night
With a rooster, a lamp, and a donkey,
And finding no lodging for any of them
Was forced to sleep in the woods.
"But all that God does is done well," he said,
Lighting his lamp to read,
While the wind blew out its flame,
And thieves ran off with his donkey,
And the rooster was chased by the fox,
But he slept with the words in his ears that night:
"All that God does is done well."
When the rabbi returned to the village to dine
He learned to his horror and surprise
That enemy soldiers had killed
All who slept in their beds that night
As he pondered his sleep in the woods,
The unlit lamp and the brayless donkey,

And the rooster not there to crow.
So the rabbi went back to the place that he knew,
Back to his town to tell,
"All that God does is mystery,
But all that God does is done well."

Prayer: Dear God, we come to You with all kinds of
questions our head does not understand,
for it is in our heart that we know that all
You do, You do well. Amen.

What Is Baptism?

"And when Jesus had been baptized, just as he came up from the water, suddenly the heavens were opened to him and he saw the Spirit of God descending like a dove and alighting on him. And a voice from heaven said, 'This is my Son, the Beloved, with whom I am well pleased.'"

Matthew 3:16-17

In your faith imagination you are seated in church. You are listening to the organ's sounds of praise, inviting everyone to worship God. Picture Jesus in the River Jordan being baptized by John the Baptist. Remember the minister placing his hand on your head and saying to the congregation, "This is God's child," and to you, "You are now a minister of God, because all of us are children of God and baptism gives us a special place where we belong and where people promise to care for one another." You stand to sing the hymn and say the prayer and the minister invites the children to the front to see the baptism of the baby. Gathered around the baptismal font, today there is a big tub of warm water. You watch the parents remove the clothing of the baby infant as the minister takes the newest member of the congregation in his arms and places the baby in the tub of warm water. The baby plays in it, and then your pastor sprinkles water over its head and says the words of baptism.* The baby is smiling as its parents dress it in baptismal clothes, celebrating God's gift of life and a holy reminder of whose we are.

BAPTISM

The father holds the baby *(rock arms)* with gentle love
    and care.
The mother stands beside them, and everybody there
Is quiet as they listen *(forefinger over lips)*
And happy *(smile)* as they see *(point to eye)*
The pastor take the baby to bless it tenderly *(hand on
    head)*
With tiny drops of water upon the baby's head *(sprinkle
    water)*,
Baptizing with special words, he says,
"God loves you, little baby, and you will always be
Within God's care, part of this church's family."[1]

Prayer: *Dear God, thank You for loving us as Your
children, for being a part of the church and of the
world You love. Amen.*

[1] Elaine M. Ward, <u>Be and Say a Fingerplay</u> (Prescott, AZ: Educational Ministries, Inc., 1982) p. 10.

Bedtime

"I think of You on my bed..."   Psalm 63:6

In your faith imagination you are getting ready to go to bed, but you do not want to. Needing a glass of milk, asking whatever questions you can think of, you try to delay your bedtime. Mother comes into the room with a book, Bedtime for Frances,[1] the story of an animal-child who does not want to go to bed. Frances needs a glass of milk, has a dozen questions, and once in bed cannot go to sleep, so she makes up an alphabet song she sings to herself, "A is for..., B is for...," and so on until "T is for tiger...," Tiger! Frances thinks about tigers, wonders about tigers, and sees a tiger in her room! Although she is not afraid, Frances thinks Mother and Father should know. Assuring Frances that her tiger is friendly, they send her back to bed, but Frances cannot sleep. She looks around the room and sees...something big and dark...a giant! "I think that giant wants to get me!" Frances finds her parents watching television and eating cake and joins them in eating. Finally Father suggests that Frances ask the giant what it wants, and to her surprise, she discovers it is no giant, but only the chair and her bathrobe. Frances returns to bed and looks up at the ceiling, thinking of all the bugs that could come out of the crack above her head. When nothing does, she notices the curtains moving by the open window. "Something is waiting..." Frances thinks. But by now Frances' parents are in bed. Father explains that as it is the wind's job to blow the curtains, it is Frances' job to sleep. Back in bed Frances hears a noise, a loud noise at the window: BUMP! THUMP! "I know something will get me!" she thinks and pulls the covers over her head. At last Frances gets up and goes to the window and there she sees...a moth! France returns to bed and sleeps, for after all the tigers, giants, moving curtains, and loud noises, Frances was tired. As Mother finishes the story, your eyes close and you sleep. Return to this place and open your eyes.

I WISH ...

Every night when it is time to sleep,
I wish I were a wooley sheep.
Sheep never have to wash their faces,
And they can wander many places.
Sheep never have to comb their hair,
or brush their teeth,
or worry what to wear,
or cover up with blankets warm,
or come inside when there's a storm,
or set the table when they eat,

their breakfast is underneath their feet.
I'd really like to be a sheep.
But if I were a sheep
I would miss
My father's morning hug,
My mother's kiss.

Prayer:

Now it's time for me to sleep,

I pray, dear God, that you will keep

Me safe within your love this night

And wake me with the morning's light.

Amen.

[1]Russell Hoban, <u>Bedtime for Frances</u> (New York: Harper & Row, 1960).

When I Am Afraid

"Teach me your way, O Lord,..."
Psalm 27:11a

In your faith imagination your stomach is upset because your stomach is a coward. When Stomach is afraid, it gets rid of all the food you have eaten. Now you feel too ill to do the thing you feared. Today is the day you have gymnasium. Because you feel awkward in gym, it seems the others laugh and make fun of you. Today is gym day and Stomach feels sick. What will you do with your fear? Finally you say to stomach, "Stomach, today you are going to gymnasium" and Stomach throws up your breakfast. You say, "Stomach, you are going to gymnasium." And when you get to the front door and Stomach tries to throw up the breakfast you didn't have, you say "Stomach, it won't do you any good, you are going to gymnasium," and you and Stomach go out the door. When you are ready, return to this place and open your eyes.

HELP ME FACE MY FEAR

One night when I was half asleep, I heard the heavens roar
And shriek, saw streaks of lightning leap, and rain began to pour.
I hid my head beneath the sheet and closed my ears up tight,
Against the frightening thunder and the noises of the night!

Then through the thunder and the light, I heard a quiet sound
And lifted up my sheet a bit to sneak a look around.
The quiet shadow crossed the room and sat down on my bed
And touched my back and spoke to me and this is what it said,

"The thunder and the rain will stop and fears will disappear,
As every day we grow to know God's love and care are here,
And I will hold your hand 'til then, so close your tired eyes,
While we will listen to the groans and moans of noisy skies."

The night my mother came to me and helped me face my fear,
I slept content because I knew my mother would be near.

Prayer: Lord, teach me Your ways. Help me remember to
ask for help when I am afraid and to be brave and
trust that You will give me good ideas about what
to do. Amen.

Let Heaven And Earth

Praise God

"Let heaven and earth praise God."
Psalm 69:34

In your faith imagination imagine your father as a preacher. Think of the fun you have with your father and one day he invites you to go with him to another city where he will be preaching. You are pleased. In the car your father, wanting to talk with you about his sermon, asked, "Where is God?" You think about how you will answer.* Then you say, "God is in heaven." Your father decides to press you a bit and says, "But people have looked up into the sky with powerful telescopes for many years and they have never seen God." "Well," you say slowly, a bit upset and worried, "God is in your heart then." Your brave father pushes further, "But people have done surgery on hearts and have never found God there either." You begin to cry because you are frustrated and your father feels guilty. Suddenly you straighten your back and speak boldly, "Well, all I know is that God was what I knew before I knew anything else." Your father is quiet, as he turns the car around to return home to rewrite his sermon, based on what you have said and you are glad you have helped. When you are ready return to this place and open your eyes.

WHAT IS REAL?

What is real The wind? A flower?
The sky of blue?
A favorite book, or one that's new?
Falling leaves on an autumn day?
The things we do? Or see? Or say?
Is God real? Are you?

Prayer: Dear God, help us be bold in knowing what is real when we cannot see or smell, hear or taste, for we know that You are with us before we "knew anything else." Amen.

What Is Pentecost?

"When the day of Pentecost had come, they were all together in one place..."

Acts 2:1-4

In your faith imagination you enter the narrow, cobblestoned street in old Jerusalem. You are nervous and excited to enter the ancient building where the friends of Jesus have gathered. They smile and ask you to come in.* As you look around the room at their faces some of them are crying, some seem frightened and ill at ease. You can tell they have come together for comfort and support from one another. They have come to hear again the story of Jesus their Christ, for they know tomorrow their own trial and tribulation will come, as one of his followers.* Suddenly the sound of a violent wind from heaven fills the room, and tongues, as of fire, appear among them, resting on each of them. They begin to speak in other languages, "on fire" with the love of God. You suddenly see people who feared all was lost are now changed.* They laugh and dance and continue to speak in different languages, filled with God's Spirit. Fifty days after the death of their leader they are now stirred to live and to die for their Christ.* You smile for you have just seen and been a part of Pentecost, the birthday of the church. Then knowing you can return to this birth of the church whenever you wish, return to this room and open your eyes.

BALLOONS AT CHURCH

"We don't bring balloons to church
Nor sing at the table
Nor wiggle in the pew.
We don't walk in the rain
Nor daydream in class. "

But we are beginning to celebrate
Children (and adults) using our imagination,
Knowing God is neither "he" nor "she,"
But the One who loves and seeks our company,
That Jesus is our friend, and the church is
Filled with singing, laughing, touching, praying,
Stories of small boys and giants,
Balloons on special Sundays,
Celebrating God's great blue balloon of Earth
And all the colors of the rainbow.

Prayer: Dear God, Spirit, Word, thank You for Your church that celebrates Your love and creation, especially the Day of Pentecost in the name of Christ. Amen.

What Happened On Good Friday?

"...'It is finished,' and he bowed his head and gave up his spirit."   *John 19:16-30*

In your faith imagination you are wandering aimlessly, weary, discouraged, concerned with some problem or injustice in the world. It is Friday, later to be called Good Friday. You come to a hill and see three crosses on which three men are hanging. You approach and stand with the people beneath one of the crosses on which is written: JESUS OF NAZARETH, THE KING OF THE JEWS. * The man is mumbling through his pain. He is telling his friend to take care of his mother. Then Jesus says, "I am thirsty" and a soldier gives him a drink from a sponge on a long stick and Jesus drinks and says, "It is accomplished," and dies.* As you cry over Jesus' death, you ask "Where is God? What has Jesus accomplished?" and give your thoughts words of thanksgiving.* Because you are in the presence of God even here at the foot of the cross, you praise God, for you know the rest of the story, and God is God.

YET— John 21:17

All their lives they had awaited your arrival
Yet
You came when you were not expected.
They visioned you with army and horses,
    a royal robe and reign
 Yet
You came as a poor peasant, a nobody from Nazareth.
Your disciples looked for a Master with a map,
a destination, and a goal
 Yet
You taught them parables they did not understand.
And we too seek meaning, healing,
    wholeness, harmony
Yet
You say to us, "Love one another
                "Turn the other cheek,"
                  "Feed my sheep."

*Prayer: Dear God, help us see through Your surprises to
You and Your plan of love for all creation. Thank
You for meaning and healing and harmony. In
the name of him who said, "Love one another"
and "Feed my sheep." Amen.*

Death

In your faith imagination enter the land of Narnia where the great Lion Aslan lives. Here Digory and Polly met the great Lion, Aslan, who represents Christ for the animal world. Digory had overheard his Aunt Letty say to a visitor who brought his dying mother some grapes, "Poor, dear Mabel! I'm afraid it would need fruit from the land of youth to help her now. Nothing in this world will do much." Digory, however, knew that there were other worlds, for he had been in one of them himself, and he began to hope. Perhaps there might be fruit in some other world that would cure his mother. He tried to ignore this hope, but he could not, and because so many odd things had happened already, it just might be true, especially when he remembered the face of Aslan. With his magic ring, Digory had returned and decided to ask the Lion for help for his invalid mother. Aslan however, had other plans for Digory. Digory was tempted to say, "I'll try to help you if you will promise to help my mother." However he realized in time that the Lion was not at all the sort of person with whom one tried to make bargains. Out of love, however, with a lump in his throat and tears in his eyes, he blurted out, "But please, please—won't you—can't you give me something that will cure Mother?" What Digory saw then surprised him as much as anything in his whole life, for when the tawny face was bent down near his own, he saw great shining tears in the Lion's eyes, so big and bright that Digory felt as if the Lion was even sorrier about his Mother than he was himself. "My son, my son," said Aslan. "I know. Grief is great. Only you and I in this land know that yet. Let us be good to one another." The Lion drew a deep breath, stooped its head even lower and gave him a Lion's kiss. And at once Digory felt that new strength and courage had gone into him. Aslan sent Digory to get an apple from a special tree far away, the Tree of Life. Digory read the silver letters on the gates of the garden where the Tree of Life grew: "Take of my fruit for others or do not take at all."[1] And though Digory was tempted to taste it himself, he brought it back to Aslan to be planted in Narnia. From the tree that grew Aslan gave him one of the apples and when his mother had eaten the apple she was well, and all was well. The doctor called it "a miracle." But Digory learned that there were worst things than losing someone you love by death. With Digory and Polly you look into the Lion's face as Aslan spoke, and feel a sweetness and power enter you that you felt you had never really been happy or alive and awake before. Now knowing you can return to Narnia whenever you wish, open your eyes and return to this place.

I WILL BE WITH YOU—Ps. 23:4

The bird will sing,
  the bird will fly,
  and some day
  the bird will die.
For that's what plants, pets, people, too,
  all living things, someday will do.
But Jesus said, and Jesus knew,
  "God promises
  "I'll always be with you!"

Prayer: Dear God, it is tempting to want to make "deals"
with You instead of praying "Thy will be done."
We thank You for stories that help us be faithful in
trusting Your love. Amen.

[1]C.S. Lewis, <u>The Magician's Nephew</u> (New York: Collier, 1974) p. 86

Why Do We Have To Die?

"Listen, I will tell you a mystery! We will not all die, but we will all be be changed..."
I Corinthians 15:51

In your faith imagination you wonder, "Why do we have to die?" and Winnie Foster enters, telling you her story:

"One very hot, dry, dull week in August when I was tired of my mother and grandmother's naggings, I was ready to run away from home. More than anything else I wanted to do something important, to be someone who mattered and took my first step toward doing something important. I went into the woods my family owned and met Jesse Tuck for the first time. There I discovered the secret of the "Tucks Everlasting." Once I knew their secret, there was nothing they could do but kidnap me. This was not what I had expected nor the way I wanted to leave home, but with time I began to enjoy the homely little house of the Tucks with its silver cobwebs and gentle dust, and the mouse who lived in the table drawer. The secret the Tucks had kept hidden for so long was that long ago they had drunk from the spring in our woods and from that day never grew older. Jesse was seventeen and one hundred and four. Of course I did not believe them. Nor could I understand why they were upset about living so long, for I preferred that no one would die. Tuck tried to explain: "It's like this rowboat," he said, as we fished. "If we didn't move it out ourselves, it would stay here forever, trying to get loose, but stuck. That's what us Tucks are, Winnie. Left behind. And everywhere around us, things are moving and growing and changing." I told him, "I don't want to die." "No, not now. Your time's not now. But dying's part of the wheel... You can't have living without dying. So you can't call it living, what we got. We just <u>are</u>, we just <u>be</u>, like rocks beside the road." That week in August I had my chance to do something that mattered and I grew up because of it, but the Tucks...they just went on...and on...and on.[1]

You thank Winnie Foster and open your eyes.

IT'S TRUE!

The joy of Easter is when we know
That God is with us and shows us so
In bird and flower, in life that's new,
In the story of Jesus that says, "It's true!"

Prayer: *Dear God, thank You for Your gift of life and new life, for Easter and the story of Jesus that says, "It's true!" In His name. Amen.*

[1] Natalie Babbitt. <u>Tuck Everlasting</u> (New York: Farrar, Straus & Giroux, 1975).

What Is Easter?

"Mary Magdalene went and said to the disciples, 'I have seen the Lord...'"

John 20:1-18

Close your eyes and enter the story in your faith imagination. It is after Jesus' death and burial. You feel the heaviness of the death and are surprised to see Peter and Jesus' beloved disciple running to the tomb where Jesus has been buried. You follow them. When the beloved disciple reaches the tomb, he looks inside. "The grave cloths are still there," he says. Peter enters the tomb and sees the grave cloths in one place and the face cloth in another, and the beloved disciple enters, looks and believes. You follow closely behind them but they cannot see you because you are seeing in your faith imagination.* When Peter and the beloved disciple return to their home, you are alone. Jesus is dead. His body is not in the tomb. You stand outside the tomb and cry.* When you look inside the tomb again, you see two angels dressed in white, one sitting at the head and the other at the feet where the body of Jesus had been. They ask you, "Why are you crying?" You reply, "They took the Lord and I do not know where they put him." Again you are asked the question, "Why are you crying? For whom are you looking?" It must be the gardener. "If you have taken him away, tell me where you have put him." The man calls you by your name and you turn and look at him.* You recognize Jesus and tell him how you feel. Do so now.* You don't really believe it is Jesus.* As you stare at him, you know it is Jesus and approach him, and he says, "Do not touch me, but go and tell my friends that I am going to my Father and your Father, my God and your God."* Then he is gone. You sit in the silence alone, in amazement, too shocked to move. Jesus is alive! Jesus is not dead!* Suddenly you jump up and run to tell the others. "I have seen the Lord! This is what he said!"* When you are ready, knowing you can return to Jesus whenever you wish, return to this place, and open your eyes.

HE LIVES!

> He Lives!
> > No grave could ever hold him fast.
> He lives!
> > While fields grow green and twilights
> > > last.
> He lives!
> > As no one else has lived before.
> He lives forever!
> > And forevermore!

Prayer: *Lord, we give You thanks for life! We give You thanks for new life! Although it is a mystery, Christ lives and we believe in his and our resurrection. In His name we pray. Amen.*

What Is Thanksgiving?

In your faith imagination it is Thanksgiving Day. You and the other children are bringing food gifts at Thanksgiving to share with others. Alice holds up a can of carrots and you all say, "Yuck!" Bill holds up his can of spinach and you all say, "Yuck!" When Beverly holds up a can of peas, you all say, "Yuck!" Steven looks up at the teacher and says, "I don't think the hungry people are going to like the food we brought."* You think about the hungry people and the food you have brought because it is Thanksgiving and the word reminds you of all the good gifts and blessings you have been given.* As you sit in the silence with your images of blessings and gifts, you talk with God, thanking God for life and love and whatever you wish to thank God for at this time.* Then, knowing you can return in your faith imagination to Thanksgiving whenever you wish, open your eyes to this place.

THANKSGIVING IS A SPECIAL DAY

Thanksgiving is a special day
That we hope never ends,
When everyone gives thanks to God
For fall and food and friends.

Prayer: *Thank You, God, for this special day, for food and friends and all good gifts, especially for Your love. Amen.*

How Can I Help?

"And now faith, hope, and love abide, these three, and the greatest of these is love."
                                        I Corinthians 13:13

In your faith imagination you meet a small boy named Wilfrid Gordon McDonald Partridge. He lives next door to an old people's home and knows all the people who live there. Wilfrid invites you to meet his favorite person, Miss Nancy Alison Delacourt Cooper, because she has four names, just as he does. Aside he whispers to you, "One day I heard my parents talking about Miss Nancy, because she had lost her memory." 'What's a memory?" I asked. My father said, "It's something you remember." I wanted to know more, so I asked my other friends at the Home and they told me that a memory is something from long ago, makes you cry, makes you laugh, is warm, and precious as gold." You say to Wilfrid, "Let's look for memories." Together you find seashells from long ago, a medal from Wilfrid's grandfather that made him cry, a puppet that made him laugh, a warm egg, and his football that was as precious as gold. Then Wilfrid invites you to go with him to call on Miss Nancy and give her each thing one by one. You watch her start to remember. She held the warm egg and told Wilfrid and you about the tiny speckled blue eggs she had once found in a bird's nest in her aunt's garden. She put the shell to her ear and remembered going to the beach by train long ago and how hot she had felt in her button-up boots. She touched the medal and talked sadly of the big brother she had loved who had gone to the war and never returned. She smiled at the puppet on strings and remembered the one she had shown to her sister, and how she had laughed with a mouth full of porridge. She bounced the football to Wilfrid and remembered the day she had met him and all the secrets they had told. And the two of them smiled and smiled because Miss Nancy's memory had been found again by a small boy, who wasn't very old either.[1] You thank Wilfrid and his friend Miss Nancy and remember and return to this place.

I'M GOING TO PAINT

I'm going to paint the sky today
And if there's room, I'll paint the sea,
And stop a raindrop too, I may,
From dripping "blue" on me.

I'm going to let the water flow
And smear the thunder that I hear
And watch the lightning come and go,
And sunshine reappear.

For feelings that are inside me
I've never had the words to say
Are pictured in this sky you see
I painted blue today.

Prayer: *Dear God, help me be as Wilfrid, loving and helping others, celebrating the feelings of joy and love I feel within. Amen.*

[1] Mem Fox, <u>Wilfrid Gordon McDonald Partridge</u> (Brooklyn, N.Y: Kane/Miller Publishers, 1985).

Why Do We Pray?

"I tell you, even though he will not get up and give him anything because he is his friend, at least because of his persistence he will get up and give him whatever he needs."

Luke 11:5-8

In your faith imagination you are one of Jesus' disciples. Jesus has just taught you "The Lord's Prayer." Then he says, "Once upon a time a man went to his friend's house at midnight. He threw a stone at his friend's window to awaken him and shouted, "Lend me three loaves of bread to feed someone who has just arrived at my home and is hungry." "Go away," the one inside said. "My door is locked. My children are in bed with me. I cannot get up and give you anything." The man outside knew what it meant to feed a stranger and to be a friend so he called again, "Friend, I have need." Because he cared about feeding the hungry one, he would not stop and called again and again until at last, because of his persistence, his friend got up and gave him what he needed." You and the other disciples are silent, thinking about the story.* Then you ask Jesus what he wants to say to you about "feeding" the hungry or being persistent in prayer.* Jesus asks, "What if God is the Good Friend who is asking you to help feed,* or what if

God is the Good Friend who gives?"* You ask yourself, "Who are my friends who would help me?" and "How am I a friend?" When you are ready, knowing that you can return to Jesus with your questions and decisions whenever you wish, return to this place and open your eyes.

BE WITH ME

> Dear God, when I hear funny noises in the night
> And see strange shadows,
> And wish with all my heart that it were light,
> Be with me.
>
> When I have dreams that frighten me,
> And hear the thunder,
> And call for Mother and my family,
> Be with me.
>
> When I'm afraid and all alone,
> And wonder what to do,
> Help me remember You
> Are with me!

Prayer: *Dear God, sometimes we forget to ask Your help or presence. Be with us and remind us to be persistent as the friend in the story. Thank You for the stories in the Bible. Amen.*